Note in a Bottle

By Cindy Leaney

Illustrated by Sue King and Peter Wilks

ROURKE CLASSROOM RESOURCES
The path to student success

Note to Parents and Teachers/Educators

Before reading: Ask your child what this book might be about. Read the title aloud together. Then ask what two sounds *o* makes in *note* and *bottle*. Remind your child to listen for those sounds in the story.

Written by Cindy Leaney
Designed by Ruth Shane
Illustrated by Sue King & Peter Wilks
Project managed by Gemma Cooper

Created and Designed by SGA and Media Management
18 High Street, Hadleigh, Suffolk, IP7 5AP, U.K.

© **2004 Rourke Classroom Resources**
P.O. Box 3328, Vero Beach
Florida, 32964, U.S.A.
Editor: Patty Whitehouse

Printed in China

ISBN   1-58952-903-0

Note in a Bottle

Come on, let's go. Get in the boat.

Okay, I'm coming. Does this boat float?

What's in that bottle? Is it a note?

it up. See what they wrote.

It's a map in some kind of code.
"Cross the pond. Go up to the top. Look
for a cobra, a fox and a toad."

Toss me the rope.
Hop over this log.
Follow that dog!

I hope we're not totally lost.
Is this the same road we just crossed?

No, it's okay. We're getting close.
"A cobra, a fox, a toad"—what does that
mean, do you suppose?

It's a code—who knows?

Oh, look. What are those?

They're rocks or fossils or something old.
They look like animals–
a fox, a cobra and a toad!

This is the spot.

What have we got?

A box full of jokes, a story and a song.

We got the code! It didn't take long.

Game time!

Match the boxes to find the jokes.

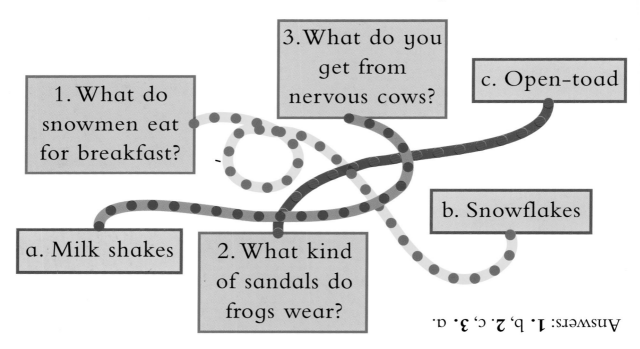

1. What do snowmen eat for breakfast?

3. What do you get from nervous cows?

c. Open-toad

a. Milk shakes

2. What kind of sandals do frogs wear?

b. Snowflakes

Can you unscramble these words?

1. oabt, 2. tdao, 3. oetn, 4. og, 5. ont, 6. ofx.